# THE COSMIC BROOM

## A TRUE STORY
## by
## ALLAN HENRY AHO

Beagle Haven Publishing Inc.
Fort Lauderdale, Florida

ISBN: 978-0-578-09968-2

# DEDICATION

*For three soaring friends*

*Eleanor Powers*

*David Parkins*

*Phil Thorpe*

# ACKNOWLEDGMENT

I would like to thank Jack Ricardo and Barbara Chadder for their able assistance in editing this book

— and —

Bill Plante for his kind words and observations while reading the manuscript

# TABLE OF CONTENTS

# INTRODUCTION

This is an account by a middle class American yacht painter and varnish man who, without any pre-knowledge or understanding of the subject matter herein described, was unexpectedly catapulted into the gentle and protective arms of reality — or what is called in the West, enlightenment. After its sudden onset, accompanied by eight hours of truly dazzling events, the mind was found to be in a life-changing and meditative state revealing insights into the conflicted mind of mankind and shedding light on the possible resolution of one's inner turmoil which can lead to a conflict free and fully awakened state.

# 1 –The Big Picture

In 1971, at the age of 33, this writer — who got his education more or less "out behind the barn" — did suddenly and of an early evening, and without any pre-knowledge or understanding whatever of the subject being written about, come upon a change of consciousness which, to use a common term, "others would kill for."

Without warning, without the use of any mind-alternating substance, this average American brain with its usual flow of daily conflicts, noise, judgments conclusions, verbalizations, tunes, impatience, anxiety, and so on, came upon a state of mind in which the brain's output, without going through any known or unconscious process whatsoever, came to a full stop. The mind and the brain became absolutely silent in an instant and without fanfare.

The flow of the usual day-to-day conditioned brain activity onto the surface of the conscious mind of which we are all familiar, had come to a complete and total stop. It took several minutes to realize that some kind of a significant change in my being had taken place.

A deep and deepening profound silence and inward peacefulness permeated the body and mind, while at the same time the audio and visual senses had sharpened to a point of extreme sensitivity.

The body had become pin-needle sensitive; not only because of what was happening in the brain alone, but because of its own inherent intelligence and its need to accommodate itself in order to express this newness.

It is not, I would say, unreasonable to have the notion that one had been catapulted into a highly awakened state, from a multi-millennium dream, for reasons which have been unexplored and remain unknown.

For about ten weeks this awakened state, this silent mind, continued day and night and produced changes in my day-to-day activities.

Included in this was a career change, which took me to a new job at a local university's foster children's care and learning center. This occurred as a natural outcome in order to accommodate the new flow of insight and value, and its natural need to express them.

A natural and high intelligence nestled in a sea of silent perception, virtue, and joy had engulfed this weary traveler, and was now on the move.

Then once again with warning not, about ten weeks later and over a 24-hour period, this new consciousness started to quickly slip away, then completely disappeared and was replaced by a darkness of all darkness, which became blacker than black. Accelerating downward, it deepened by the hour and seemed like the final moments on a hideous and pain-ridden death bed.

The blackness was silent and penetrating, even vibrating the body as it sought to adjust once again to a dramatic change, and to its core, both body and mind were hopelessly ensnared in its paralyzing grip.

While speaking with others in the parking lot, the voice seemed separated from the body as if it were coming from light years away. It seemed as if one was being overcome by the shadow of death itself, as there were images of being attached to a gigantic anchor about to be cast into the great depths of a bottomless sea.

Weary and completely exhausted from this day of battle, I was forced into an early and longer than normal deep sleep. Upon waking, it seemed that something had been settled; something had been worked out and I was free of the darkness.

As it is with all things of this world, that state of mind, which seemed to have been swallowed up by one of Stephen Hawking's black holes, had come to an end and there was a new light in the brain with a gentle, sober, and welcoming idea: "Allan, it's time to go paint a boat."

This is the true story of a typical and average middle class American man with a less-than-average high school education who suddenly and without warning came upon a phenomenon referred to in the West as "enlightenment."

I have spent most of my life as a yacht refinisher in Newburyport, Massachusetts, and for the last 40 years in Fort Lauderdale, Florida, where I continue today running a small business specializing in yacht varnish work.

# 2 – Onset of Light

There was nothing particularly different that day or that evening as I left the parking lot of the shopping center in the middle of town and proceeded to walk across the way to my newly hand-painted and shiny two-tone 1958 Chevrolet. The usual output from the noisy brain was there, as it had been for the past 33 years of this somewhat neurotic and confused life.

With the key turned in the ignition of the eight cylinder Chevy, it started as usual, but the sound of the engine was decidedly different.

I sat there quietly taking in something quite new. Normally this 283 V-8 was well-tuned and quiet while idling, but I began to notice various natural sounds from the machine and curiously began to be able to separate and tune into a particular sound.

First and most prominently, I noticed the sound of the tappets. There are two tappets for each of the eight cylinders — sixteen in all — and they are an adjustable, spring-loaded affair which are attached to a rocker arm which extend the length of the eight cylinder engine on each side. These produce a click, a tap, and a snapping noise, and with sixteen of them going off at various stages of their cycle to lift and close the intake and exhaust valves, it produced a symphony of euphonious and inviting sounds to my apparently new capacity to hear detail, and did so with the great precision of a finely tuned orchestra.

I sat there for some time listening, fascinated at this strange, new, crisp quality of the sounds, and to other sounds while observing other cars and people walking by, feeling quite at ease and peaceful — a peacefulness the likes of which I had never before experienced.

Looking back, it seems reasonable that one would be surprised or excited or perhaps question what it was that was happening. But at that time the thinking brain did not want to take part in what was happening.

The sun had just set and streetlights and the neon signs at storefronts were coming on as I pulled out of the parking lot in Wilton Manors to head home to the boat that I lived on in Fort Lauderdale, which was docked at a yacht yard where I worked as a yacht painter and varnish man.

Just out of the parking lot I came to the first traffic light and noticed that the colors red, green, and yellow had a newness to them; which is to say they were more brilliant, more solid, and there was an added sparkle to the colors, as if some new quality in the colors had come into being, never seen before this day.

Along the way during these first few minutes of driving south on Route One, the storefront neon signs, the lampposts, the people and the way they walked with their unique individual gaits, the leaves on the trees, the overflowing dumpster with the trash cascading into the gutter, the pink and fading light patches on the west side of a lonely cloud, the frown on the face of the driver to the left...all things had been cleansed, somehow renewed. Everything was clearly being seen for the first time with a different eye, a different perception; a clear eye that was not contaminated by many thousands of yesterdays.

And as one would later find out, what was happening was not an illusion, not a mental imbalance or fluke of nature, not a mind trick nor a hallucination. Quite simply, it was a view of things as they are; things as they *actually are.*

One was simply looking at life as it was happening *now*, without a reference point, without any background, without acceptance or denial, without any point of view, neither the good or the bad; therefore, without the movement of a conditioned response, without the movement or action of time or memory.

Reality had come into being, into focus. The truth of the moment was at hand and presenting itself, and so strangely so suddenly, without warning, without desire, without preconceived knowledge of its existence or even its possibility, and all of this, uninvited.

There arose a thumping sensation emanating throughout the body and flowing from the brain — a lifting up, an elevating of sorts as I pulled off the road into a parking area suspecting that perhaps the heart or something was not as it should be.

There was an actual and tangible feeling in the brain itself that something was moving about, something was being rearranged, something was changing or being taken away, or added to.

I looked in the mirror and touched my nose, then wiggled my toes to be sure that I was there. Oh, I was there all right, indeed there. I knew my name, and was familiar with my surroundings. I knew where I was going, and which boat I'd be working with on the morrow, and strangely this newness was now being quickly fueled with an increasing energy from a knowingly inexhaustible source from without.

I say *knowingly* because the proof comes with the goods! There is no question about it. It reminds me of how one frame of an old movie clip contains 99 percent picture on the celluloid, then going from top to bottom is a thin wiggly line which contains the soundtrack. With this current happening herein being described, there is the picture — the body and mind event being described; then there is this thin wiggly line of nonverbal understanding, which actually is intelligence, which is truth, running simultaneously in the background, which says among other things that one knows, and one knows that one knows. That's as close as I can get to it.

There was then no doubt that a truly concrete, and in truth a normal condition, had come into operation, quite possibly an evolutionary jump. Nevertheless and simply put, one had come home — I mean really home — and as it turns out, it was only for a 10-week visit!

# 3 – Life Without Time

The heart was not as it should be — not the beating one, not the physical one. Rather, the inner one; the one that songs are written about, the place where joy and bliss are found, the heart that loves, the heart that breaks.

Sitting there again with the engine idling, there came what I imagine would normally be called a startling conclusion. However, it was not startling at all because there was no one present to be startled! There was only this attentive awareness, this state of seeing and being.

The center, that thing we always refer to as *I*, that core, the director, the decider, the commander, the self-centered entity, just was not there, was not participating in this newness. Here, the reader will encounter the first of many contradictory, though hopefully explainable, realizations.

Quite simply put, the past, the repetition, the past conclusions, the judgments, the opinions, the comparing, the constant chatterbox brain, the totally conditioned content of the brain (except for its technological content), had ceased to function as it had in the past. It had come to a full stop.

With a very alert brain and with keen perception, the past (including the center, the *I*, the me) had ceased to function and was put aside. It ceased to be the filter through which daily life is experienced and therefore revealed a view of life as it actually was from one minute to the next, and while seeing what was happening, that previously noisy brain had gone quiet; it had become absolutely silent automatically on its own, without any invitation, without any effort, without any previous knowledge of such a possibility.

Without any knowledge of meditation, it had been thrust into what is now known to be a truly meditative state, alive in a different dimension, a place where time was *not;* again, for reasons which remain unknown.

The change which had been going on for the past half hour or so was really a revolution in the way that the brain/mind was working, and to try to explain it so that it is understandable is a particularly difficult task because it would seem to require the use of two languages. One language using thought, and one using perception or no thought, and of course this is not possible because perceptions explained become thought once again, therefore memory, and again the past. With words I cannot bring anyone inside this timeless event, but only through words (time) can it be talked around and about and if lucky, help bring one to the door. It is for the reader, standing alone and silent, for whom that door will open.

It is my assessment that what is about to be said has been said for the past five thousand years in many poetic and mysterious ways.

This is nothing new, only that this particular presentation is a product of the modern world. With the beauty of the poetry and the mystery put on the sidelines for the moment, with this laser-point attempt to create an understanding which may be more necessary than ever in this unsettling time when the bomb is sitting there, the earth's environment for the past several years seems to be screaming out a message to us by setting new records for this and that throughout the world nearly every month. If the past three years of environmental chaos has a built-in momentum, then I wonder what the next ten years are going to bring?

Over the years we have seen the

talking heads on television talking faster and faster, being downright rude and insulting; talking over each other with meaningless greetings, exploding egos, and destructive competitiveness; tripping over words; gasping for breath under the pressure to keep the cover-up alive, and woe be to he who permits two seconds of dead airtime in which a wakeup call may slip in. Without a room full of glowing pastel butterflies on chamomile tea, I honestly don't know how some of them sleep at night!

The primary purpose of this writer is an attempt to bring to light — to bring into focus — some undeniable and obvious realities in a no-nonsense way.

There is another way to try to make this understandable, and that is to watch the output of the brain; watch the thinking process of the brain, which is functioning in time — to watch it for yourself, and withhold all judgment so that you can learn for yourself. You can learn and you then can see for yourself that the past memories of the brain are contaminating, and coloring, and influencing, and distorting your present moment. This activity goes on throughout the day and we accept it as a natural fact of life without ever questioning whether it absolutely has to be this way. I say it does not have to be this way.

This watching, this attention, without any comment, without any judging, with no labeling, with no action at all by the one attending to the flowing output from the brain, sets up the potential for a truly significant discovery, and a learning experience of the highest value.

I am asserting that attention itself, as a starting point, is as well its own ending point and contains within itself a complete and full action, which is an action without time, a timeless action in the same place where all creation takes place, all newness and learning happens, and is therefore the most valuable tool in the mental economy.

Anything from the conditioned brain which passes across the screen of this timeless space can be brought to its knees and be, without your help or interference, disarmed, rendered *non compos mentis* through the spontaneous and motiveless action of attention alone. This is a tangible and seeable fact.

Timelessness cannot be achieved, arrived at, cannot be hunted down, nor acquired, as it is present now as the *now* and can be seen now because it is simply there, its observable, it came with the package, which is you.

It was there when you were born and will be there when you are gone. It is part of the completeness that you are, right there staring at you, almost looking at you, but few as yet realize it.

This timelessness is itself that space between any two thoughts, and is that place where the past as it comes into view can be challenged and neutralized, which then gives way to the new, as the seed from a dying plant delivers.

This approach most certainly can take place if one has the passionate interest to want to know and learn about oneself and this most delicate mental transaction. After all, that content of consciousness is you, put together by you, and you are responsible for it. What is in there is producing what is now the outcome of your life, and will continue to produce right to the grave.

Then, having come to this point, you can begin to see the action of a brain beginning to operate in a new, a different, and refreshing way; a way in which it is seeing life clearly without the presence or actions of yesterday, and without the movement of time.

When such a change happens, your technological knowledge, how to do your work, and the mechanics of life each day remain intact, in great detail, and more vividly as the time-bound conflicts gradually slip away.

We all know that chronological time by the clock exists to help create order on the planet. In the brain there is psychological time as the past, where all of our technological knowledge and personal psychological knowledge, along with its emotional content, is stored as memory in our brain cells.

In day-to-day living we use that past, and we have access to the present, which is the now, which has the quality of being empty. That space between every thought, that quality of emptiness, is a constant and is always there. Then there is the unknown future into which we project an idea.

That future idea, that idea of something new that gets projected into the future, is and has to be produced by thought, which is memory, which remains the past, and continues to be old. It is difficult to understand that there is no such thing as new thought. Therefore, that which is projected into the future is still the old — which, however, can be modified as the result of additional thinking.

If there is to be anything truly, creatively new, it can be found only in the now, somewhat outside of the box, so to speak. I say "outside" because most of us are not cognizant of the now and its second-to-second existence, to say nothing of its supreme value in supporting good mental health.

It is only in that place between thoughts where intelligence and its great treasures reside, quietly waiting to be discovered. It is also the place where you, the troublemaker, if he would just get out of the way, make the discovery that this is where truth lies.

The past, which is always memory, is filled with our individual conditioning created by ourselves and our surroundings and environment, and also created by that which was forced upon us by others when we were nonverbal children.

There are, as well, nondescript feelings which were registered in the brain before we had the capacity to convert those feelings into thoughts which then could be verbalized. Whether we are aware of it or not, this content of memory is being continually modified, changed, things added to, things taken away as an ongoing process during the day, and by night through dreams. There is an ongoing exchange between that which is on the surface and that which is in the deeper layers of consciousness.

We have to start where we are when

looking at what is happening on the surface of the mind. As we give attention to the activity on the surface, and seeing that activity slipping away, there becomes less on that surface and it is natural that deeper layers of issues begin to rise to the top, filling in the newly created empty space. The more issues that come to the surface and get put into the spotlight of attention, the burning laser of attention, the greater the flow from below.

It is natural for the brain to want to do this because it is natural for the brain to want to be peaceful, not to waste energy in battle. It wants to be at rest. In this new restful state the brain becomes a high-performance conduit for intelligence, which is not knowledge, and which is not yours. It's as simple as that.

Each waking day every word, every action, every thought is each moment cast into what I see as the war zone; a cauldron of discontent and turmoil, which, when some kind of crisis or new event occurs, is always at the ready and inevitably springs into action and destroys the truth of the moment.

This spring-loaded material jumps into the battle just a millisecond  before a new, truly creative condition has the potential to present itself. In this way, that which is about to be or could be new fails to get its chance because the past springs so quickly into action, and is evaluating the new according to the old; and, as earlier stated, then once again becomes the filter through which the new is then untimely contaminated. The same old battles continue, and you go round and round in circles for most of your life, then back into the grave again.

Some of what is being stated here is repetitious, and being that the fleeting details seem to be difficult to grasp for some, they are nevertheless from time to time presented in a slightly different way, or approached from a different angle in hopes that the reader's interest can be successfully accommodated.

Then we have the future, which one can project an idea into. In everyday life we use our technological memories to deal with the mechanics of life; how to do our job, drive a car, pay the bills and such. We also have psychological memories with emotional content, and when confronted with something new — such as meeting a new person, for example — we generally and unknowingly meet that challenge with a great lack of clarity because our conditioned past is always there in place, and while not realizing it, that past then acts by judging and evaluating with the old and then applies that to the new and fresh challenge.

We end up facing the new challenge with the old, with old history and old baggage, with old memories running in the background, and then the games begin.

Everything is on the move. Evolution is happening now. Evolution of the brain is ongoing and the evolution of consciousness and group consciousness is in constant flux, and here we are, for the most part anchored in the past with not much of a toolkit to face the ever-present realities of life and change, both on the inside of our head and the outside world around us.

# 4 – The Yacht Yard

It was becoming late now, and being satisfied with a minor and silent review of what was happening, I turned the key in the Chevy once again and proceeded down Route One toward the river and the yacht yard, which was nestled in a very nice and quiet neighborhood.

It was a Monday night and extra quiet because it was known as "recovery night" by the locals; that is to say the resident workers who worked for the yard and who lived on the boats docked there, and the temporary visitors who were the owners of vessels currently being worked on.

There were families with their children, preparing for a winter of cruising the Bahamas or deeper into the Caribbean.

Each year there would be at least one family high on their dream, preparing to sail around the world, as well as local yacht owners doing their annual maintenance, and crew members from the many American corporate yachts that were being worked on.

Over the five years I spent working at this yacht yard, there was a cast of real characters from around the world who would appear, then disappear down the river a few months later after their work was done. Returning to the open ocean, some would return the following year with their new stories of high seas adventure, embellished, of course, on Saturday nights when eight-foot waves gradually grew to eighteen, and a thirty-five-mile-an-hour winds became a sixty-mile-an-hour howling gale. Fueled by Caribbean rum, the later the night, the higher the sea, the stronger the wind, the bigger the me!

Then there was the rare case of the

yacht that headed for the open sea for the last time, never to be seen again, only to encounter a final tragedy.

There was a real family atmosphere there, and in the evenings and on weekends there were cookouts under the giant mango tree and, needless to say, in the true American yachting tradition, the beer and the wine and the Hudson Bay and Caribbean Rum were in free flow, especially on the weekends. Thus "recovery Monday" and its extra quiet evening.

This evening, rather than park close to my boat, I parked at the far end of the lot, wanting to slowly walk the full length of the facility. Consciousness was still elevating, ratcheting up, expanding as borders in the brain itself kept pushing out, then falling away, creating a vast space. It would be satisfied for the time-being as it established a new boundary.

It was two o'clock in the morning and

the stillness both in the mind and outwardly had a great depth. Everything was asleep save for the river as it moved swiftly to the sea, making an occasional rustling sound as it wrapped itself around the many pilings of the boat shed on its way back to the sea.

The more open one becomes, the greater the vulnerability, the bigger the heart, the stronger the joy, and the more cutting is the pain while looking at life. There is suffering all about and we are the masters of cover-up.

The greatest security in life comes with the complete abandonment of what we see as security. What we see as security must be continually reinforced, and even then it will fail over time. The abandonment of psychological security brings one to a natural and infallible cosmic security.

Over eons of time through the

building of man there has been put into place all that is needed to find a joyful, meaningful, and peaceful life. That thing to be found is not at the view of a magnificent mountain range, although it could be; not in the serenity of some mystical spot on the earth, although it could be; but right where one is, right here, right now, and only right here and right now. In that *now* space is that which is eternal and is ever-present.

There was an increasing lack of resistance while the body was in motion. Gravity itself was shedding some of its normal grip and I was feeling an increasing weightlessness.

There was a very long boat shed that ran the length of the parking lot and opened at both ends. It was a giant roof really, with walkways on either side of each bay and its bays were full of all kinds of boats from many ports which had recently arrived from up north to enjoy the comforts of the Fort Lauderdale winter, and to engage the expertise of the many fine craftsmen who worked there at Summerfield Boat Works.

Everything, of course, was familiar as I had mentioned before, and all of my necessary technological knowledge and that of the mechanics of life and the ability to communicate and learn do survive the otherwise clean sweep of the cosmic broom. With all past psychological conditioning, along with its emotional content put aside, the world is now seen as it is for the first time with a new cleaned and polished lens of both the inner and outer eye.

The visual perception, including that of the unseen, is a kind of high definition that will never be discovered or formulated by the investigators and the detectives of the material world, nor will it ever reach the shelves of Best Buy, as this is the activity of the unknown, the thing that time cannot touch, and that which man has been in search of for many thousands of years.

Passing the boat sheds, the weight of the body was just barely detectable as I moved through the open air joiner and carpentry shop, engine mechanics and welding shops, all silent now, at rest in the middle of the night awaiting the noise and activity of the day to come in just a few more hours. The brain also was silent as not one single word or thought had passed this awake observer for several hours now.

I picked up a piece of newly cut cedar wood being used by a carpenter who was in the process of lining a closet in a large yacht with its beauty and fragrance. The off white, yellows, the pastel pink and reds, along with the grain in the wood, had over many years spun themselves into a tapestry, a piece of artwork which will deliver for many years, then slowly decay back into the earth and back to its source.

All things of the earth are united, connected, and one. For many this remains just a theory. Man has separated himself from his true identity and all things of the earth, and has done so in his head through the evolution of this illusionary thing called *I*. He projects this powerful *I* with its data of yesterday's old and dead memories outwardly into the world which he sees. This act or action produces an imminent distortion of reality (truth), and prevents him from seeing what the actual facts of the moment are.

What is on the outside is always pure and clear, but what he sees on the outside is colored, distorted, and filtered by that which is on the inside. The inside is his content of consciousness, his memory, already past, already yesterday's judgments and conclusions, already old, already dead.

If there be a storm on the inside of the mind, that storm will then be the setup for a storm on the outside. If there be corruption on the inside, it will play out into the world through his behavior and his actions on the outside.

This enormous mess in the brain of the individual is dominated and controlled by this thing, this dominating controller, this decider we call *I*. This *I* believes that he, or she, is separate from its content and is in control of that content, and this is just not so. It is not true. It is a real illusion born of thought.

The truth of it is this *I*, this dominating idea who has separated himself from his content, has unknowingly established himself as in charge of the self, which is perhaps the greatest developmental error in the long history and evolution of consciousness.

That *I* is actually just another factor in this mix, just another part of this content of consciousness, another player in this sea of discontent and not at all separated from it except for the idea of being separate.

This belief, this idea of being separate, has created all of one's personal conflict inwardly, then outwardly all of the conflicts in the world. One's personal battles in life have the exact same fundamental causes as the battles between nations, which have been going on throughout our known history.

Should your own light go on, and you actually see this fact and take it to heart, it will irreversibly alter your life for the rest of your days!

Most of us human beings all around the world are profoundly unique and are not aware of it, but are quite alike in that we all have to deal on a daily basis with a long list of problematic and conflicting problems. No matter what country, what climate, what race, what belief or non-belief system, whether rich or poor or in between, we are all facing the same lack of harmony in our existence. It seems reasonable to assume that most all humans with a healthy brain would, as they grow and develop, aspire to the idea of having a peaceful and happy and comfortable life. It seems to me that it would be difficult to dispute this.

It also is reasonable to assume that resentments, jealously, anger, frustration, pride, attachments, dependency, loss, impatience, fear, greed, envy, suffering, loneliness, stress, competitiveness, fearful attachment to some philosophical authority, and a host of other issues dominate each day and we are in battle with this accumulated debris all of our lives.

Body language is to me quite profound, as it speaks louder than the tongue. Sitting on a bench near a corner, watching the faces of passersby and the drivers waiting for the red to go to green, I have not been overwhelmed by happiness. The children, on the other hand, perhaps under five years of age and not yet contaminated, deliver a joy which one joins in on and produces nearly a tearful response.

All of this is draining away our energy, going around and around in circles, perhaps finding a solution at times, or checking out the many self-help books in the marketplace these days. Having made certain discoveries, this writer claims to have seen certain solutions which are ever-present right here, right now, and staring at us at every moment of every day.

# 5 – The Cosmic Broom

Standing in the open carpentry shop I could see my boat at the dock, which was surrounded by at least a dozen large sailing yachts secured two and three abreast out into the river, their tall masts reaching for the blue-black sky with fluffy billowing white clouds riding the gentle southeast breeze. Some clouds were expanding as others were dissipating depending on their encounter with wispy tongues of drier air.

All things of the world are in constant movement, constant flux, constant change while most of us remain centered to the self and anchored in yesterday. This was truly a Renoir moment; this was Monet live.

The old brain could never see this sight and no description could ever touch it.

For there to be a description there would have to be a describer and the describer was not, as he had been swept away earlier in the evening. Thought is the creator of the *I*. Although it may be difficult to understand, this *I* is the greatest illusion ever put together by the mind of man. It has brought us to a sorrowful, and increasingly sorrowful state, especially so in this modern time.

What was being seen that night was truth, reality, things as they are, a result only of a state, only of a dimension in which time does not exist. A timeless state, which has a quality of supreme fragility and delicacy which thought will destroy in an instant. A state in which the *I* and its content must be laid to rest, put aside, in order for this newness to be.

I leave two night lights on at night in the old '42 Elco sedan cruiser, which was built of wood in about 1946. A white one in the main salon and a red one down below and forward. This night the lights shone through the portholes and windows like a jewel with a soft invitation to join.

I stood there at the end of the dock looking out at the boats and the river, which was again moving rather swiftly as it sought to equalize itself with the level of the sea a few miles to the east, then rest a while before giving in once again to the endless demands of the moon.

The silent, empty brain was quivering with life, dancing with joy. It was happy to be still and relieved to be free of the battle, to be naturally quiet, and empty for perhaps the first time in many thousands of years.

Then out of nowhere, quite suddenly the body started to feel the movement of gravity returning, and just as quickly fear was taking up residence in the stomach and began pumping into the body as if by a large dynamo. Sensing some kind of event or some kind of possible danger, I boarded the Elco and entered the salon and remained standing there just inside the cabin door as the fear grew to a monstrous level.

The heart was beating wildly, palms were wet and the legs seemed ready to collapse. I was shaking under the weight of this thing, this growing and swiftly moving burden. Though I had the urge to escape, and could easily have done so, I knew unquestionably that the coming storm had to be weathered, the lion had to roar, the beast had to be permitted to express itself.

Fear is a living thing, and if there be intelligence it demands one's full attention. Fear wants a response. It wants you to do battle with it in order to maintain itself, to survive in order to stay sharp and alive, and it must do so in order for it to fulfill itself. By fulfilling itself, you permit it to continue as well as strengthen.

I just stood there knowing the necessity of it, knowing this thing had its mission. It continued to bang its head against this immovable one who would not give in, who would not even acknowledge the word *fear*, who would stand there in a deep and stunning silence, permitting this thing to act out its punishing ways. It may not seem believable, but to even inwardly call this feeling fear would be a move away from its purity. It is the purity which provides the clean sweep, the complete action, as only awareness was happening.

After some unknown period of time it grew tired, it gave in, seeing it could not succeed, could not get through, could not get the acknowledgement it fed on and needed for its life, for its survival.

The house was empty now, and the one who would acknowledge once again had been swept away hours ago. This thing named *fear*, it collapsed dead to the deck, as all organic things will do in the end. Then it disappeared; it withered away like a drought-ridden dandelion in the blazing sun, revealing at last what it was covering up, for that was its job, to escape from, defend, to protect, to cover up.

Thought is an organic process, a product of time, stored in destructible brain cells. Emotions, stored as they are in the brain cells, are also a material process. There is nothing of the spirit here. Nothing, including *thinking* itself.

Emotionalism is a response to feeling, and being a step away from feeling, it remains an escape from feeling, and even could be said to be a defensive action in place so as to prevent the movement of feeling, which has purity, beauty, and depth, when it can stand alone unprotected.

When emotionalism is permitted to

run its course, without being steered or re-routed by desire, then the purity and depth of the feeling, which is the root cause, will come through clearly, thoroughly, and intensely. It is this purity that, if left to express itself in silence, will bring a final end to the problem and deliver a new measure of freedom to the mind, giving added space and a increased volume of energy.

To believe this or not to believe this are equal mistakes. It is only this action, a product of a truly courageous and attentive state, which will bring about this complete action, the complete and total destruction of this problem.

A mutation in the brain had taken place as fear died, leaving only a disarmed intellectual hulk in a trace of memory.

The fear, which had fallen away, then gave rise to a greater peacefulness in the new and continuing silence. The body was gaining strength in preparation for the onslaught which was sensed to be in the very air one was breathing. The atmosphere was electric; there was real magic in the air.

Moments later, standing there with a silent, empty, vibrant and attentive mind, it came.

In a flash, that which had been covered up by fear pierced through the breathless silence, as images from the past were projected on the wide screen of the empty mind and started flying by, not unlike comets and cruise missiles, at a very high rate of speed, in color and in white and black, with frozen, pain-riddled stills and fast-forward tumbling splashes of hideous images from past nightmares. Thunderous herds of gigantic elephants chasing and stomping the boy down on the streets, on the Hill of the Goats. It was Hollywood's best; it was Caesar's Show of Shows. I stood there like a bronze of

Custer viewing these vivid images of the past.

There must have been many thousands of them, including odors which were present during certain past events and traumas, and bodily pains like being hit and punched and kicked and torn, and with tears and moans, the images in stark and incredible crystal clear Blue Ray detail continued pouring in, accelerating, then slowing, resting a second or two only to race forward once again.

In mental anguish and with pain and loss and suffering, the toys of the child ripped and torn away then burst open once again, and laid it all out, skipping not a beat, leaving not a frame nor a portion thereof on the cutting room floor. The pain and shock of it all was gently acknowledged and clearly recognized, fully understood as I silently bade goodbye as this non-me, who in absolute and thunderous silence, continued to stand there unmoved and stunningly cognizant.

So cleansing and pure was its aftermath, like an all-night steady rain on a dusty town that greets a new morning like no other, blanketed with a new and glistening sun.

Although it may appear so, one cannot get away with anything in this world. The truth will be faced either now or later, and like it or not it will be faced. It seems that there are certain laws in place in nature and when they are not adhered to — whether one knows of them or not, whether they are understood or not — the piper will be paid, the learning and life will go on.

Standing there in the salon there was a newer brightness all around. It was now after three a.m. and the consciousness had been in real and full meditation for nearly eight hours, and now as a result of what had just transpired, was again expanding in an explosive and deep silence beyond the previously established borders set only an hour or so ago.

I had to be at work just one hundred yards away in a few hours, and did not go down below to the bunk in the forward part of the cruiser, but rather lay out on the large and firm old leather couch in the main salon.

This long day did not require a review and the body went instantly to sleep as if it were that of "Bond, James Bond" who, as you may recall, would in his hotel room do battle with the bad guy, take him out, then fall instantly asleep!

Although my habit was to lie on my side, this night there was an inward demand to lie on my back with arms at my sides. At the moment of falling asleep, it was noted that three separate things were going on.

It would perhaps not hold up in

court, but I would still testify that there were three entities in the salon at this time. The body was asleep, that was for sure. The consciousness was clearly apart from the body and from above was watching with some kind of affectionate care for just a moment or so, then it disappeared.

Today, sitting here writing some 42 years later, I do not know where it went. Just the other night I had a dream that it went off to visit with Doctor Who and his friends Sara, Romana, Adrick, and K-9 (thank heavens for K-9) for a ride in the type-forty Tardis! In the dream I did not tell anyone on board, but I was hoping that we would encounter Darvos, the truly evilest of evil arch-enemies of the Doctor's and find a way once and for all to dispose of the dreaded Darliks! Would that have been real, it sure would have been fun. I've always liked the Doctor of the '80s and his friends.

Then there was something else directly associated with the body and separate from the mind. It was located there, by the sleeping body's side, and appeared in some way to be tethered to it. There was a sensation that it was a guide, or a protector of some kind, something of another related, although independent and currently yet to be discovered, system in life.

Also, I do not know where the awareness of this sensation had its origin, but there is, or rather I suspect that the body actually has its own intelligence system of some kind which likely includes some level of awareness, something that helps to sustain it while it is in a crisis of some kind and when it has no access to its mainframe; that is, no access to the consciousness which is normally associated with it. If this turns out to actually be the case, then it may help to explain how some individuals survive in situations that just simply seem impossible and the experts cannot explain, such as coming up dead from one thing or another, and being so for nearly an hour, then suddenly springing back to life.

As the body slept, a pure energy poured into it through the nostrils and also much more strongly and with great volume in through the toes. It was a vigorous flow and the body was experiencing the flow and was well aware of the moving of this energy through itself as it lay there in silence. The body was the one acknowledging this fact, although its owner was off on holiday.

There are two uses of the natural energy that I am aware of, and the one that most of us are familiar with is the energy which supports our life as lived in the field of time; that is, the day-to-day existence with its conflicts and stress, the happy times, and its sorrows, the pleasure and the pain which are constantly being produced by memory, which is the past. And of course, that energy is renewed during sleep. If one is having a bad night due to excessive conflict, then naturally you will awaken to find that your energy has been dissipated as a result of the battle.

Also, if one is having a dull, lazy, quiet day, for example, then suddenly there comes a crisis like your boss calls to tell you that you're fired, that nervous energy kicks in and gets strong as it tries to find a solution to the new crisis after the cursing stage has passed. But because this new crisis is a product of time and has its roots in thought and the past, then it soon wears one down and quickly becomes exhausting.

The energy flowing into the body this early morning was at the full, and is the same energy and from the same source as is used by a human being who is living in the world of time.

Being a product of the master builder of the *all*, it is not only inexhaustible, but it regenerates and replenishes itself *as* it is being used, not *after* it has been used. There is no gap between its use and its regeneration.

I had slept for less than three hours, and as soon as I awoke, the body was fully awake. There was no hangover so to speak, as there would be if the brain had been in battle in the night trying to bring a resolution to the many incomplete transactions of the day, and the duel of the opposites from the many yesterdays.

The inside corners of the eyes did not accumulate any of what is called "sleep crusty." One awoke one hundred percent, fully clear, energized and on the move.

By the way, an incomplete trans-action can be as simple as having dropped something on the floor, then noticing it and knowing that it would be best to pick it up but not doing so. The brain then records this little incident, and adds it to the content, thus adding to conflict and further reducing space in the brain by just a hair.

So, this night after the clean sweep of the cosmic broom, this writer entertained for the first time the dreamless sleep which would continue for the next ten weeks or so.

# 6 – Free of Yesterday

ork began at 7:30 a.m. and the thirty or so workers ranging in age from 18 to 70, along with the general manager, gathered in the open air woodworking shop which was the center of all yard activities. It was a bustling, entertaining, and overall pleasant place to work.

The management was good to the workers, and the manager was an open, intelligent, and knowledgeable man and was a friend to all. He ran the place with what seemed to me to be great ease, skill, a keen eye, solid judgment, with far-reaching yacht maintenance skills, and was a deliverer of fairness to all he engaged.

He would mingle with the guys in the morning, as there was always some local gossip flying about. Then at 7:30 every day for years he would yell out, saying, "OK, let's go, let's go."

The machinery would fire up, the air compressor would start banging away, and the mast crane would send up a puff of smoke as its diesel spread its resonance over and about the eastern third of the yard. The workday was off and running.

I was one of six members of the paint crew, which had a foreman. We usually would be working on several yachts at a time so that with various jobs in progress we could bring one to completion in the most favorable of weather conditions at the time.

Straight away, the paint foreman would delegate the various jobs for the day to each of us in the paint crew. Standing there on this first full day with a fresh, new and empty consciousness in this group of men, all of whom I had known fairly well for about three years, I noticed as one sort of bulk observation that all of the opinions and judgments which I had previously stored in my brain about these co-workers quite simply were not there. The slate had been wiped clean. My relationship to all of them was completely new and free of the past.

Do bear in mind that all of the technological knowledge about these people remains intact. All this is needed to properly relate to, and interact, and is necessary to get along and relate to the world, and presently to get the job done, so to speak. These memories are, I might add, very vivid now, very sharp, and one has greater access to them with the newly cleared and cleansed brain.

It is the psychological memories, the knowledge, the previous assessments and opinions and judgments about a person which present the problem. The past praises or criticisms, the likes or the dislikes I had of this person, whether having been jealous or envious of this person in the past, my view, my opinion of the goodness or lack thereof of this person in the past, are a perfect illustration of what time is, and what prevents a true and clear relationship. This person is by far more than the blanket I have wrapped him up in.

I think it is easy to see this self-created trap we have built! Locking in these memories of times past, times which instantly and automatically come into play at every engagement, contaminate the *now* instantly, and cancel out any possibility of clarity, or of anything new.

This *now* is the only place in our mental economy where there is the possibility to discover the new, and so long as this old conditioning functions, we cannot be free of conflict; we cannot know a peaceful day. This is what it's like for all of us every day as we move closer to the grave, repeating again and again, with only an occasional insight into something new.

Then at some time of the day, if you go into a room and meditate with any kind of effort and try to find something that someone told you is supposed to be there, or to bring about a quietness as an end result of meditation, you'll find it is quite far removed from reality. If there is any effort at all or any movement from a center as the *me* or *I,* which is trying to gain or acquire something, then it will always fail because the *I* is the invention of thought. Some meditation teachings actually work this way and are popular, and unfortunately create a result which is not true.

If the *I* stops being active, there will still be a vibrant human being who will freely live without a center. It is possible just to sit without a motive and just watch to see what happens and not take a part in the activity. To observe and do nothing else, you will see that the action will subside and quietness will naturally present itself.

I'm quite lucky that no one ever suggested that I meditate, which is in many forms just an unintended and unrealized expansion of ego and the suppression of thinking and noise. Anything which is suppressed will come back. Thought can end naturally and will end naturally when there is simply a state of attention. Attention alone without taking any action at all will cause the mind to become quiet naturally. This is an observable fact which can be tested and seen. When there is this attention, there is no *I* or *me* attending.

There is, however, nothing wrong with spontaneously sitting and watching the activities of the brain. Watching without taking action, rejecting nothing, accepting nothing, just watching, just seeing what is there. Looking, not for something, but just for its own sake, just seeing with a gentle intention to learn, with no motive to gain or to gather.

# 7 – The Boy

The boy was all of seven or eight years old and living on the Hill of the Goats; that is, Goat Hill in Beverly, Massachusetts. I happen to remember seeing the last of the goats on the hill in probably 1942 or 1943.

On this particular morning while walking to the Edwards Elementary School, a nearly half-mile walk from my home, I started to feel an urge, an inward demand to stop in the center of the span of the Boston and Maine rail trestle and look south down the center of the tracks in the direction of Boston.

This was not a fearful or foreboding feeling or anything like that, just an urge, just a sort of inward, nonverbal demand to do it, so I proceeded casually and approached the center of the span and looked south. There was simply an introduction to the understanding that "there is no death." It was not a voice from the outside or a voice of authority, nor was it a voice from the inside. There was no voice at all, but rather an acknowledgment from the mind, perhaps an inward and silent reminder of what was always known. That's it, that's all.

The response was instantaneous, the feeling was blasé, lacking any futuristic significance. I was indifferent, as if to say, "Well great, kid, that's fine. So now tell me something I don't know."

That feeling recorded well and came back to me the other day and is available and as strong today as it had been that morning sixty and five years ago. I turned and proceeded to school without another thought about this incident for many decades.

Growing up on the Hill, I would say

that I was as normal as any of the other kids, and there were lots of them from many different ethnic backgrounds. There were lots of stories, one of which is now vivid.

While quite young, a girl from across the way and I used to conduct elaborate funerals for birds that would turn up dead in the yard. We would place their bodies in silk-lined caskets which were fashioned of old discarded eyeglass cases, of which there were many in our cellars. The bird would lie in state for a time, and sometimes the ceremony would not be held till the next day when she would hum some kind of music, and with flowers and all, the deceased would be laid to rest in our bird cemetery. We did this dozens of times slowly, with a prayer, flowers and all, as the casket was slowly lowered six or eight inches into the welcoming earth.

We spread the funeral out over a two-day period because that's what the adults did on the Hill where there were many wakes in the living rooms of the deceased.

I went to a number of them myself, always alone, and the bodies were always near the bay or front living room windows and on each side of the casket in those days there were two tall lamps with upside-down purple globes (supplied by the local funeral parlor) reaching for the heavens and casting a strange light in the room, causing the flowers to take on an unnatural hue.

There was, I thought, something comforting and maybe a little exhilarating about the color purple in this setting and I thought that if I ever got to go to a magic carpet store, I'd order a carpet that was predominantly purple, thinking that maybe it would go a little faster than the others.

One day when all the old-timers from Finland were drinking coffee from a saucer for cooling, and with a solid block of sugar in hand in the faraway kitchen, I snuck into a living room as I wanted to touch the face of the dead distant great grand someone or another, and did so and became quite alarmed because his face had turned to cement. I then darted out the open front door and flew up into the giant old cherry tree where I sat for a while quite unimpressed.

I've been looking at many of the old childhood photos as of late and they all show a very happy child.

Around age fourteen or so something gradually started to change and I began not sleeping well and would be up into the night thinking of questions which I would like to have answers to.

At about that same time I joined the Sea Scouts, which is a branch of the Boy Scouts of America. I had that interest because I was interested in boating and did have a small boat on the river, a sea skiff, which was used to set and haul lobster traps in the Danvers River, which surrounded and wrapped its gentleness quite nicely around the Hill of the Goats.

A license was required to lobster; that is, to go lobstering, and that trade was closely regulated by the state even at that time, back in the early '50s. I sold the catch on the Hill for about four years, and in addition made Christmas wreaths to sell in the winter. Also, with a paper route, I was self-supporting and gathering self-reliance at an early age and had a tendency to want to be in charge of things — to be the boss.

A first notable mental conflict started to emerge as I was about to enter high school when my father, Henry, and my Uncle Walter started to inject the idea that I should be on the high school football team.

I remember that they approached me rather hesitantly, on several occasions. I gathered that perhaps they were suspicious that they were about to be treading on thin ice.

They had another brother, my Uncle Al, who was known as "The Flying Finn" back in the day, and a high school football hero of sorts at that. I suspect they wanted to relive the old glory days once again through me.

"The Finn" means Finish; that is, from Finland. I have always liked and preferred the Finish part of my background and still regard myself as being fifty-one percent Finnish, and as far as I know, and to their great credit, Finland may have been the only country to pay in full its war debt to the U.S. of A.

I was waffling for a month or so about this football thing trying to figure out how to get out of this one, or not committing to this completely unpalatable proposal. I could not quite imagine a 125-pound skinny kid on a football team.

So this conflict was cast into the mix of these increasing philosophical questions that were floating around in my brain and keeping me awake at night.

My father and uncle put pressure on me about this issue quite frequently, but it was, I think, a not too unreasonable and perhaps somewhat normal and acceptable level given the times and the fact that we are all locked into the field of time and do often live in, and want to relive, the glorious past rather than face the now, which is for the most part quite the battleground for many, filled with peril, and increasingly so these days, with its flashes of certain truths which may slip in from time to time.

My weight was 125 pounds, as stated, and has been maintained for the past fifty-eight years. I don't think I would have stood up very well on a football field despite the fact that I was athletic, a bit of a competitive sailboat racer, and a good baseball player, and may even have been as fast as a Finn could be. Fast around the bases, good in the outfield, I could also hit home runs in the neighborhood lot.

Well, the answer came to me one hot summer morning when I decided to find out what the trade school had to offer. So I trotted down there hoping for a good outcome and checked out the scheduling relationship with the high school program, and football practice times. The news was great.

Based on what I think I was told, I figured that if I had chosen the trade-school route, I would not be able to go to football practice because of the timing, as the trade school ran later in the day than did the high school, and also I would strive to keep my high school grades as low as possible, which was not difficult for the likes of me. After all, I was getting some education out behind the barn!

I was rather pleased with my clever and broad-based plan because it further reduced the possibility of future threats to my independence, and sort of, I felt, covered all the bases.

I'm not very sure that a trade school kid could be on the team, but I implied this to be so, and presented this "Joe Friday" scenario (just the facts) in such a creative way so as to keep the lid on and prevent any kind of investigative reporting, keeping in mind here that all of the bones in my body were on the line.

I think that I had attributed some of this cleverness to lessons learned a few years back, having had my ear every night glued to the radio listening to "Nick Carter Master Detective" and "The Shadow," who, by the way, assured me that "the weed of crime bears bitter fruit." The Shadow knows! It's like something is watching us all the time, and indeed there may very well be!

This also reminds me of another radio hero. From the studios of WBZ Boston, Carl Desuse would brighten the mindscape every morning with his dry Yankee humor and hit tunes of the day. My favorite segment of that morning show was "...And now a word from the philosopher's handbook." He would come up with something quite interesting every morning with a nice lesson in life as an attachment.

I thought it was quite nice and that perhaps I would do the same someday. That is, have a radio show, write my own philosopher's handbook, and sort of be like Carl Desuse. I even went so far as to drive into Boston to a broadcasting school for the voice version of a screen test.

They told me that I had a great radio voice and when they played the tape back to me I had reason to agree. Then they told me the cost of going to the school. Ten thousand dollars! So that was the end of that dream.

So one fine morning, and with some degree of boosted confidence, I finally announced my decision after having signed up for the print shop training program at the trade school. I did this before telling anyone so as to lock it in place, hoping it would be less likely to be a matter for further negotiation.

My mother, father, and uncle were all in the room. I was leaning against a door frame in the kitchen with hands folded in front of me and I do believe exuding a new confidence while making the announcement. It stayed a bit quiet, as everyone was disappointed, and I kept hidden my joy for what a clever plan I had come up with.

The enemy was deflated. My father, who had a rather passive nature, especially in a crisis, did not pounce. I was happy to be the winner in this and had some enthusiasm at the thought of becoming a printer, as I was interested in becoming a printing press operator, having a bent toward clicking and snapping machinery.

After starting trade school, I took to driving my new, jet black Bel Air Chevrolet late into the night northward into the hills and valleys of Southern New Hampshire and Maine, and sometimes as far north as Frighberg, Maine. Driving for hours on end and at times returning at three in the morning, I would often be asked, "Where have you been?" "Out," I'd say. That's what many of the kids said back in the '50s. I did this through all the seasons at least two nights a week for years and years with the dedication of the postmen of the day, through wind and rain and all the rest of it.

Being on the road and in the car driving seemed to produce a comforting and favorable atmosphere for what was going on in my head.

The long and winding empty country roads seemed to give license to a long and winding and endless thought process. There was a certain freedom in it, a certain pleasure in chewing on even discomforting things. Knowing that there were miles and hours ahead was sort of comforting, but any resolutions were few and far between.

The thinking machine by now was revving up and was in a routine which would go on for many years. The questions went on and on and were mostly of a philosophical nature. I could not make sense of the differences which divided various groups of people in the world. It seemed to me that if everyone shared the same basic outcome of life — that is, they are born, grow and have various universal conflicts, age, come upon failing health and die regardless of what they believe in — I suspected that there had to be a universal and common consequence to the ending of life regardless of the variety of belief systems.

There were the everyday conflicts, of course, that we all experience, usually associated with relationships with the people with whom we work with at our jobs and the family battles and mini-battles. Wanting to do this or that and not being able to. Wanting to purchase something and not being able to come up with the cash.

I think the reader knows what I'm talking about. Much of this sort of thing is going on with you, right here and right now. I did have some degree of luck in this area as I seemed to get along pretty well with most people, as my father did, and was quite the observer of others conflicts from a safe distance. It seemed to be easy to understand what was going on with them, but to myself I was my own mystery man.

Being rather quiet on the outside and somewhat distant with others, I was always trying to figure what was going on with the other guy while the building storm clouds in my own mind were slowly forming an eye.

Issues within personal relationships were also in the mix, and in addition to having a girlfriend, there was also a boyfriend. This pattern continued with myself and other acquaintances as the decades moved on. With decreasing attention given, this issue is now seen for what it is, as being a fact of life which runs throughout nature.

Not unlike the wake left by a sleek, fine sailing yacht which melts into the sea, the relationships always ended smoothly with nary a trace of debris.

The affairs were of good quality and honesty, with hardly ever a harsh word, and they all gradually came to a smooth, agreeable and natural end.

There was one little incident, however, in Florida, involving a third party which constitutes a triangle of sorts, and being naïve and a bit careless at the time led me to believe that there was a strong likelihood I could end up in a barrel of cement at the bottom of the gulf stream. I was a beer and wine drinker at the time, but not to any great excess, and I recall shifting to a firm Canadian whiskey for the duration as I tried to wiggle my way out of that one.

It seems a bit surprising to me as I look back upon it that there could be good, relatively conflict-free relationships happening and at the same time have this racing, introspective brain. I guess that I was good at separating these two aspects of my life and, come to think of it, the older I got the more I tuned into the philosophical nature of the brain and its content.

The definition of love, or what love actually is, has been an ongoing thread of inquiry for six decades. There have been times when I thought I had a grasp of it, and very clearly so. That was while one was in the timeless state, that fully awake state of conscious where the past does not interfere with the pristine clarity and joy of emptiness.

One could write a great deal about emptiness if only there were a very large non-word dictionary, its contents of which could be drawn upon.

It seems to me even now that much of what we call "love" in personal relation-ships is very much rooted in the silent images of yesterday's happenings, and if we are honest with ourselves, we gradually see these images, like everything around us, slipping away and turning to ashes.

Love can only be now, as living is only now, and the truth of my being is only now. Yesterday is dead as a door nail, tomorrow may never come, and if one could gently slip into the natural silence of life for just a moment or so, one could see that *now* is where it's at; *now* is undeniably ever-present. *Now* is forever; it is eternal life, and love is eternal, love is *now*, not to be attained somewhere in a new tomorrow which may never come.

One also cannot deny this genuine soul mate situation, love at first sight, a strong and meaningful bond that often goes on to the end. There seems to be some merit there. There have been many situations like this among public notables and scattered, I'm sure, throughout the general population. I myself have had a brush with it and tend to believe that these types of relationships have their roots in the very distant past, in other times, in other lives.

Despite a very conflicted mind on the surface, I have generally felt that I came into the world with a somewhat stable and grounded constitution, with a good dose of logic and reason, the product of an ancient past from which one has gathered the tools now being sharpened to weather any storm.

Even today I suspect that there is a rather large and quiet underground revolution of mindfulness permeating all societies on the planet, and despite the current fray, it will slowly wiggle to the surface and cast its shadow and then its light, and make its mark even with perhaps some pretty rough times coming down the road.

There are, of course, some joys and pleasures in life for most of us, however fleeting, and some people actually like their jobs, and some do have good and sound relationships.

I was lucky in that respect, despite the fact that I did not care for being indoors. I enjoyed the work as a printer running these productive machines, and I enjoyed especially my fifty years in boating-related work, which included some real seagoing adventures.

However, I believe for me the serious philosophical questions which would pop up in my head carried the greatest burden. With the little I knew about things, there were some things the local Sunday school authorities tried to teach me which simply made no sense to me at all.

I had no inward or outward opposition, I simply and passively followed the rules and would show up each Sunday knowing the day would come when I would be free of it.

This stuff had not a chance with me anyway, because for me it just went in one ear and out the other. Well, not altogether true. It did go in one ear, but by nature I was "stone deaf" in the other ear, so the material going in had to make a u-turn when it reached the "stone" in order to get out again. This created somewhat of a traffic jam at the good entrance and just added to my mounting confusion.

I also used to think about the earth, to some extent. Here we are crawling all over the planet and we find everything we need to get along, as it seems to have been set up this way.

Shelters are there or can be assembled. Out of the ground comes the grasses for bread, the fruit, the rain, nuts, and the sun, and roots and tubers and vegetables, all of which sustain health quite nicely I find. There was no such thing as a Twinkie tree, a burger bush, or the Big Gulp waterfall.

We have now two colossal diseases on the move in this country today, diabetes and obesity, both of which are completely and totally preventable! Think of it. Completely and totally preventable! We do not all need to be scientists to understand this.

If we know what the cause is and that information is stuck in the intellectual portion of the brain, nothing will happen! The intellect on its own can be filled and overflowing with cool and calculating accurate information, but it does not create! It is only when that information reaches and combines with the heart that there is the possibility of a creative action. A single interested politician who is "heartfelt" regarding this issue should be able to produce a worthwhile and workable approach to the problem.

Costing billions of dollars each year, and with the future projected numbers, it is a staggering challenge in itself, enough so as to make other natural crises which are moving our way — and with increasing momentum, I suspect — more difficult to financially deal with.

Someone should be getting the message out. This whole issue, like others, seems to be trapped in a news cycle, with an occasional flurry when a new and more staggering report comes out.

Then it disappears, covered over by the latest gossip about someone's new baby. We are, it seems, so immature with our heads buried in technology and entertainment. I think someone is going to have to wake up and smell the roses, the scent of which may already be fading.

# 8 – Aloft

Early on, working for this boat yard, I developed a specialty assignment which most painters were not terribly excited to take on. This was varnishing ships' wheels, which were rather intricate and required a good deal of attention and patience, and a quiet, out of the way place away from the radio and other distractions.

The other was varnishing the tall masts of sailboats while the masts were in the boat and at the dock. This was a tedious job in which a man on deck would control a hand-operated winch with a braking device, and by using the wire normally used to raise the sails, haul me up to the top of the mast while sitting in a canvas sling called a boatswain's chair.

In addition to being in the chair, I

also had tools with me; scrapers, sand paper, cleaning fluid, rags and so forth, and after the preparation was done (which could take a day) I would then, the next day, go up again with the wet varnish and brushes and cleaning rags and while slowly being lowered by a hopefully competent and attentive winch operator, produce a nice, clean, and sparkling job which would generally be good for a year or so before failing due to the persistent tropical sun and salt air.

In New England you could get away with two years, but here in Florida the sun with its strong ultraviolet rays does quite a job on the old-fashioned, oil-based varnish, and a vertical surface could last for about a year before needing to be redone.

I always enjoyed arriving at the very top of the mast where my eyes would be above the top of the spar and one was able to see the surroundings, the river, the passing yachts, the sky, and the swaying palms without obstruction.

Suspended there in space some sixty feet above the deck it was peaceful all around and away from the busy activity and noisy world below. One is really alone there, but not lonely. No talking because no one would hear, except for the occasional yell to lower the chair a few feet as the worked progressed.

I used to spend some time looking closely at the earth and seeing that it is abundant with life. There were tiny creatures everywhere — visible, to say nothing of the invisible.

From aloft much more area was seen and each palm tree must have had hundreds of thousands of ants alone, and the river was full of life as was the grass and its creatures and the many weeds, all with something to do, as they are there not by accident.

When we walk on the earth we

destroy much life and it is natural to do so, but it matters not because where there is life there is always life. You cannot put it out, for when the time is right, no matter what, it will just spring back again, fresh and new, with another chance as it continues on its way.

Strangely, it seems that if you could put a scale under the corner store and take its weight — and we will say, for example, that it weighs in at one hundred million pounds — then set it all alight and bring it to the ground in a pile of rubble and ash, then put it on the scale once again, it would weigh in at one hundred million pounds again provided that you could put a container over the fire and capture all of the residue and let it settle, including the smoke. Nothing is ever lost. Nothing. It just appears to be that way.

# 9 – Gates of Heaven

Several days after the dramatic events which occurred while the consciousness was expanding, things seemed to level off and it would appear that there was not going to be any further change. I continued to work at the yacht yard for another two weeks, and during this time the mind was sparkling clear and efficient during the day with almost no accumulation of memory, and the dreamless sleep at night was the new normal. While the body was asleep it was aware that it was alone without its consciousness, and also aware of the pure energy flowing into the body, and in my case flowing in through the feet and nostrils.

When the brain is fully awake and attentive during the day it does not accumulate as it had in the past, except when it has to, especially when it has to do with new mechanical or technical knowledge, which needs to be saved. Because of this, I have very limited memory of many of the things that occurred during this ten-week period.

I had become aware of a position for a shop instructor at a children's rehabilitation center which was being funded and managed by a local university. After being interviewed, I started right away and moved onto the university grounds where several nearby houses had been purchased for the learning center. I was given one half of a house along with the garage, which I converted for a woodworking and house repair shop. The center, which was waiting for a renewal of funding from a federal grant, was low on funds at this time, and I purchased the tools and equipment myself to get things started, and was to be reimbursed after the grant went through.

In addition to being a shop instructor, I had the job of transporting students to various appointments with doctors and psychologists in the county.

I noticed from the start that there were many paid professionals and volunteers in this program, which had only about a dozen or fifteen students. At one time I did an approximate estimate of the cost per student, and although I do not recall the figure, it was very high and seemed quite unreasonable and perhaps not sustainable.

These kids were just disruptive enough not to be able to be in the public school system, but not bad enough to be in any kind of detention situation. The learning center was designed to bridge the gap and to restore the students to a degree of stability so that they could return home and to a normal school environment.

On this particular morning, upon

wakening, the mind had an extremely sharp edge to it, very deep and electric and quite possibly something had occurred in the night, although there was no sense that anything unusual had happened. This morning I was to take two of the boys from the school and drop them off at some kind of testing facility about fifteen miles away from the learning center.

As mentioned earlier, the silent mind had been stable for the past six weeks or so. By that I mean that there had been no dramatic events, just a quiet, extremely alert, sensitive, peaceful, and happy brain remained present. No past memories ever interfered with the challenges of the *now* during this period and attentiveness, which had become a daily, nonjudgmental, constant state, prevented any accumulateing debris from entering one's once noisy day-to-day existence.

After dropping the boys off I sought out back roads and neighborhoods to drive through on my way back to the center, because I wanted to drive as slowly as possible, having an inward need to do so given the high sensitivity of this morning's consciousness. There was a feeling that something out of the ordinary was in the making.

As I drove along, the penetrating silence of this morning's mind was slowly deepening in a very soft, gentle, and almost affectionate way as if there were something present, comforting and guiding me and at the same time exuding somewhat of a gift-giving nature.

One could actually feel the established borders of the silent brain once again gently cascading, falling away, almost in slow motion over an imaginary edge into an endless abyss, tumbling downward through blue-black space forever, while at the same time consciousness was smoothly expanding into a silent, explosive nothingness, filled with everything, filled with all that there is. The space around myself disappeared completely, leaving no borders, no resistance. One was freer than free, immersed namelessly in the all of the all.

The freedom could not be measured, and the body was weightless as something new and never seen was on the move, and the body, fully aware and capable, did safely continue to drive the automobile, while at the same time the driver was soaring. (Others have reported this fact, that driving and meditation can indeed happen at the same time and with safety.)

I admit that it may be difficult to believe that being in a state of absolute and full meditation and driving an automobile at the same time may seem to be quite incompatible; nevertheless, it was so, as the evolution of consciousness seems quite capable of accommodating itself to the modern world as it likely did in the distant past.

At the final approach to the school property and on a country road with cattle grazing in a large open field on this brilliant Florida winter day, I pulled to the side of the road and turned off the engine.

The audio nerve in my left ear, which had been diagnosed years ago as being dead from birth, had been vibrating for a while and had become very pronounced in its physical sensations. It occurred to me while sitting there that my hearing was about to be restored. This idea brought about a tinge of fear accompanied by a fear of the degree of power which was being exhibited at this time.

There was also a quick flashback of my mother and father driving me to Canada at the age of twelve to try to get my hearing restored as the result of visiting the shrine of Saint Anne de Beaupré. The cathedral had the inside walls nearly covered with wheelchairs, crutches, and other medical support devices displayed as testimony of what was possible. As for myself, I walked in stone deaf in the left ear and walked out the same.

A restoration or healing of the left ear did not happen at this time because of this element of fear, as I call it, and perhaps a whisper of doubt which at the time I preferred to keep. There was a certain resistance and a feeling of not wanting this action to go forward.

There must be absolute openness for such an occurrence to take place. Although I believe I had the understanding as to how this could be brought about, I was hesitant to touch it, partially due to a high level of virtue which accompanied my particular case of enlightenment, as well as a genuine lack of interest in phenomena which I see as being a reality as well as a distraction from what is more important. It seemed that my particular focus was the ending of mental turmoil and the freeing of the mind to then make it available to the realities of the beyond.

All the activity of this day had brought myself, this grain of sand in a borderless universe, to a high point of illumination which was completely remote from thought.

I wanted to be standing, so I got out of the car and started slowly walking in the adjacent field. Although the interpretation of what happened next could be called extremely dramatic, it was not so, again due to this state in which there was no one there to dramatize. I can only say that the door to eternity had been opened and what could be seen beyond this door in a flash, then lasting some time, has forever left its gentle, irreversible, and permanent mark. One look through this door brought supreme clarity to the all of life and persistent questioning which has been going on in my head for years and years, which neither time, disease, or death can take away. That which was seen could never be put into words and this ultimate reality is there for all. We were all born with the potential to come upon this timeless dimension. The platform for its being is with us all the time and resides in the space between thoughts.

There have been times, while in a daydream, I have called upon a stranger, saying, "Hey, you, sir, come this way. I want to show you something."

Just take a look at this magnificent machine, so strong and powerful. Fashioned of New England oak and locust, and varnished up like the yacht of a very rich and famous man, I would like to place thee in the sling of this grand trebuchet and then catapult thee out of this field of time and into the other world where time is not, so you can see for yourself what I see — for only five seconds or ten — and upon landing, see the look on your face and know that you have seen the all and have not a question to ask, as it really would be that way.

Returning to the Living and Learning Center late in the afternoon, this high, this deep penetration into another dimension lasted through the night and into the following day, and was the epitome of all the things which had taken place over the past ten weeks.

It has only been ten thousand years since man left the nomadic times in the dust and civilization has come into existence. Civilization being the end of nomadic life, the building of the first cities, the domestication of animals, and the beginnings of agriculture, all of which happened quickly between (according to the fossil record) only nine to eleven thousand years ago.

A few thousand years after that, there appeared the early sages and teachers in northern India, along with the formation of the great philosophical and belief systems and organizations which exist today. Many of the old ways and writings and the beauty of it seem to be cloaked in mystery and ritual, and likely will be further clarified as the new age of enlightenment progresses.

It seems reasonable to me that a truthful message should be fairly easy to understand by the average person with a healthy learning potential. Maybe it is as simple as that. All information and teaching was indeed suited for its time and would, or should, evolve with the times, and maybe that is what is starting to happen at the present time.

# 10 – Diagram of Consciousness

The illustration appearing at the end of this chapter represents the consciousness of any individual human. There are only four parts illustrated. The top area with the solid dots represents the very conscious part of the everyday mind of man. The professionals are in general agreement that, like an iceberg, about ninety percent is hidden and we are aware of only about ten percent of our content of consciousness.

The next layer can be described as sort of a battleground where the content of each area is constantly exchanging information in the form of thoughts, ideas, confusions, contradictory views of one's personal life, images, theories, wide-ranging fears and facts, daily problems, and fantasies, etc.

There is also, for example, the shifting contents of ongoing resentments and other mental battles which you are chewing over and at times deriving some pleasure from, and this activity goes on and on both day and night.

The larger area shown, filled with circles, is the hidden. All of the above is in there, along with childhood traumas (both verbal and nonverbal), pure pain, a variety of nervous and defensive habits, and the copious details surrounding the hidden and not so hidden fears, as well as the blocks which you have established and fearfully entertain which prevent you from having a clear and happy life, and also prevent you from discovering the beauty and creative genius which resides within.

This stuff goes round and round, decade after decade, and then finally right back into the box you go once again, following Jack Horkheimer's suggestion, and you just keep looking up!

There is also the ancient past, and at the bottom of the hidden area, and in the deepest layers are rooted, imbedded, difficult and painful and highly emotionally charged areas such as the roots of addiction, attachments, and dependencies. These cause you to bargain with and to cleverly manipulate friends and lovers, and all the others, in order to keep yourself in what you believe is a safe area to protect yourself from the suffering which is inherent with the prospect of loss.

There has to be the generation of courage to be and remain in contact with this highly and emotionally charged baggage. To remain in contact with this stuff is the key to its absolute and guaranteed destruction.

To believe what has just been said will continue your paralysis. To disbelieve it will continue your paralysis. But to do it is your non-way way to the discovery of its truth. Non-way because if you have a way, that would imply that you, the *I,* would be carrying this out.

It is the attentiveness which carries this out, which produces the action, and that attentiveness is not your possession. That attentiveness is the eternal friend! The guru, the teacher you have been looking for while jumping from one book to another, one organization to another. That teacher is right where you are, right here, right now. Others have said: "Know thyself" and "To thy own self be true."

You don't have to face this alone. There is a sentry at the gate of consciousness; the greater friend is always there. The greater friend is always there to melt into. The greater friend is the seer, the looker, that which is attending, the laser, the unknown. It is the one without time, the nameless, the eternal. It is the cosmic broom, it is the *I* less one which acts, the *you* that is true, the true you.

A meditative mind is necessary during the day to come to understand what you are all about. Then below this, for illustration purposes, is the absolute, the Waterford clarity, truth in all things, the greater friend, vivid reality, a freedom unimaginable, a creative intelligence which is not yours, and which can change *your* world, which can change *the* world.

Also within this clarity may be found the bag of tricks, psychokinesis, the bending of metal with mental power; and what is currently called ESP, extra sensory perception, which then becomes no longer extra; taking egotistical advantage of losing gravity. Such phenomena may be entertaining and fun, but to me are quite valueless.

True meditation, what I call the real meditation happening in the day-to-day life, watching without recording, without pride which separates you from the world, without judging, is a sure way out of the mess that we are in.

Once underway by a committed individual who is seriously interested in solving the mystery of life and who is really doing it, you will find that the thinking process will slowly begin to slow down. Today you may notice that the brain is extremely quick in moving from one thing to another. Meditation will slow this process naturally, and the act of looking will have a tendency to bring about an increased space between thoughts and an overall improved atmosphere about yourself.

I must admit that this *is* serious business. The attempt at explanation is complex and somewhat taxing to the brain, but there be no need to drive yourself crazy. Approach this thing gently, with ease. Call it, and feel it if you will, **meditation light** and if you are interested, gather your intention to investigate. The meaning of the word "intention" to me is subtle but strong, distant yet inwardly assertive, yet lacking ego. Simply be the *I,* lost in a thick Maine coast sea fog.

If you are fortunate enough to completely disarm the content, then there becomes the possibility that the door to all that there is will open to this quiet and silent mind, which no longer has a center, which is now free of the *I.*

What may be seen from this point will be the product of an individual uniqueness which is not the yours you knew, which is its own treasure and becomes shared with and enhances the group consciousness of the world and will help change the world.

This is it in a nut shell

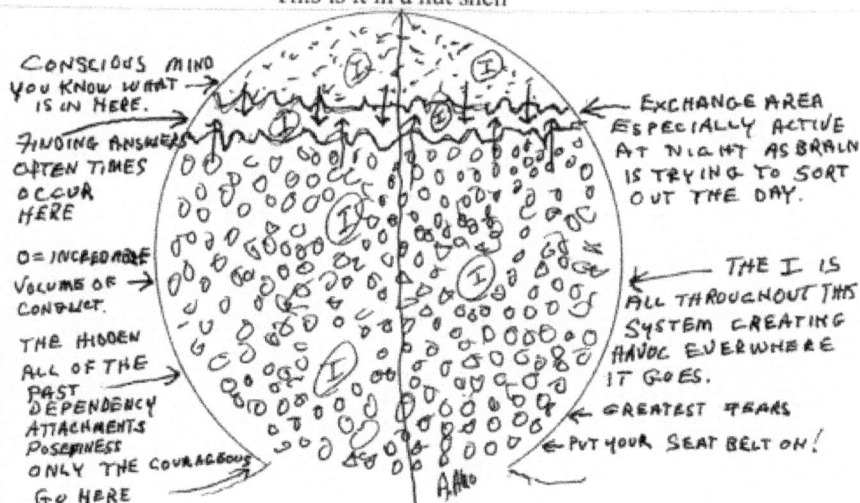

CONSCIOUS MIND
YOU KNOW WHAT → 
IS IN HERE.

FINDING ANSWERS
OFTEN TIMES
OCCUR
HERE

O = INCREDIBLE
VOLUMS OF →
CONFLICT.

THE HIDDEN
ALL OF THE →
PAST
DEPENDENCY
ATTACHMENTS
POSERSINESS
ONLY THE COURAGEOUS
GO HERE

← EXCHANGE AREA
ESPECIALLY ACTIVE
AT NIGHT AS BRAIN
IS TRYING TO SORT
OUT THE DAY.

← THE I IS
ALL THROUGHOUT THIS
SYSTEM CREATING
HAVOC EVERWHERE
IT GOES.

← GREATEST FEARS
← PUT YOUR SEAT BELT ON!

Borderless vastness

It is natural for this to assend

True intelligence (not yours)

will enter when you get out of the way

let go, let the greater friend enter, be

it's ready when you are

ENLIGHTENMENT

The world needs you now

Let your blinders slip away, this is really simple stuff

# 11 – Lights out

There was some sense of instability at the school regarding funding and grant money, which had been going on from the time of my employment. There was a general fear that the program had become too expensive, and that the grant perhaps would not come through. There was a large staff of professionals and volunteers, and many staff meetings to document the activities of the program, as there was this grant proposal or renewal in the works and in need of being successful as the deadline was fast approaching.

About three days after having a look through the doors of eternity there came a troubling night of listlessness and loss of sleep, and I suspect that dreaming may have started once again after ten weeks of day and nighttime bliss.

I awoke this morning with a feeling of pure dread. The first thing I noticed was that thinking had partially resumed and conflict had restarted, as was my general past history. I was not capable of observing, of giving my attention to what was happening. As each hour of the morning went by I continued to be sinking into a depressive state of mind and could not grasp any tool to deal with what was happening. Hour by hour the degree of decline accelerated as the workings of the cosmic broom collapsed in upon itself. What was going on in my mind was, by noon, completely out of control in that nothing could be done to reverse the decline of the cosmic sense which had been running the show for the past ten weeks.

By late afternoon my mind had entered a darkness to outdo any dread imaginable. Blacker than black and accelerating downward, it deepened by the hour and the body seemed somehow to be separated from the mind. Even my thinking voice had been separated from the body. It was like the final moments on what could be described as a pain-ridden deathbed.

The blackness was silent and penetrating, even vibrating the body as it sought to find some kind of comfort in this rapid and dramatic change. Both body and mind were hopelessly ensnared in its paralyzing grip. Overcome by a great and heavy tiredness, and feeling that the shadow of death itself was hanging over me, I slept for many hours as the brain tried to come to some resolution to this frightening conflict.

In the morning I awoke with a great heaviness and feeling that I had been in an epic battle for life itself. The heaviness lifted quickly and I was aware that there was no disappointment or regret about what had just transpired, what had been lost. I was feeling surprisingly clear. There was no interest even in thinking about it. Then all at once there was light in the form of an idea. There was a comfortable view of the future and I simply said to myself, "Allan, it's time to go paint a boat!"

# 12 – Aftermath

When I left the boatyard to work at the Learning Center, I had put the boat that I lived on up for sale. Fortunately for me it did not sell and no one even looked at it. Consequently, when I got my old job back I simply moved back onto the boat at the yard and everything was back to where it was prior to the onset of the new consciousness, about eleven weeks earlier.

I did not have any regrets over the loss of that new state of mind and did not even think much about what had happened, although there was a reconditioning that I had come upon, something quite significant, and having seen what I had seen, there was a solid understanding and a resolution to the important philosophical questions that had been before me for many years.

Even though I had spent ten weeks with a meditative state of mind being a way of life, it would take several years for me to start to learn — or to re-learn — what meditation really was while once again living in time where most of my daily activities are colored and filtered by yesterday's memories.

One of my friends, a ship carpenter who also lived on his sailboat with his wife and two children, was known to have had some interesting experiences. He was known in his native Canada and in South Florida as the "man with the healing hands." He told me that he was working on a mental healing project.

At this time there was a serious palm tree disease sweeping the South Florida area called "lethal yellowing" and he said that he was doing what he called "spiritual mind treatment" on several of the local palms, and that it was successful in treating and reversing the disease process. He was also successful in healing serious physical problems in humans which were brought to his attention.

One day I told him a little about what had happened to me, as I was wondering if he had an opinion as to the reason why someone like myself, who had no knowledge or experience in these spiritual matters such as himself, would come upon the intensity of events which had occurred to me. He simply said, "My friend, you are an old soul!" It was left at that.

Some years later I was given a so-called "psychic reading" as a gift from a friend. I did not know this lady and had never spoken to her. She was two thousand miles away and was given only my name and location. The gift was in the form of a forty-five-minute cassette tape. There was a good deal of accuracy in what she said, and some errors, but she also mentioned that I had been around for a very long time and that I was an old soul!

Several months had gone by and before long I began to realize that I was becoming discontented with my work at the yard and felt that perhaps I could do better. I started giving some thought to branching out on my own and starting my own business working out of the trunk of my car doing yacht refinishing with a particular interest in specializing in varnish work.

I certainly did not find any encouragement about this idea from the people around me, and especially from the other painters in the paint crew. It was actually quite a frightening idea to start out with such an entrepreneurial idea, having had no experience in dealing with people in that role. I did, however, have some confidence in being able to produce quality work.

What I did was to write an

introductory letter about my now ten-year experience as a yacht refinisher and hand delivered it to about fifteen different yacht broker agencies who were in touch with individual yacht owners, to let them know that I was available for such work as a freelancer at a price far reduced from the yacht yard services.

To myself, I wrote down a list of about eight principles which I believed were good guidelines in dealing with customers which would assure a successful relationship with them and a successful business. I gave my notice to leave the yard once again, and on the final day I had projected that the phone would ring and that my first job would come in, that afternoon of that last day that is exactly what happened.

From that time forward, the business grew by word of mouth and gained momentum until I had two employees for nearly twenty-five years, and as I reached my mid-sixties the work gradually started naturally to taper off until today, at seventy-three, I still have several yachts which I take care off.

During the first ten years or so after I returned to boat work I was visited by the Cosmic sense one or two times a year. This would always happen unexpectedly while working, driving the car, or even washing dishes. There was only one time which lasted about two hours, but most others were a minute to perhaps ten.

During this time I also started reading on this subject and discovered that there have been many individuals, some famous, who have had this cosmic sense throughout their lives. It was discovered that oftentimes these people were of a religious nature and some had studied Eastern religion and various meditation practices. The optimal age for the onset of enlightenment seems to be between thirty and thirty-five years, as it was in my case.

Others have reported only a very brief encounter, which did not maintain itself but produced a major, permanent, and positive change in their lives.

There was one particular event worth going into detail about. Returning home from a job one particular day, I was noticing the movement of unusually strong fear during the last fifteen minutes of the drive. It seemed kind of strange to me, because I was not aware of any particular issue going on which would produce this intense feeling, as I was quite stable and reasonably happy. The fear increased as I approached the house and upon opening the door, the fear would subside and stop after I had been in the house a few minutes. The following day it would start in again around the same time and was a bit stronger than the day before, and it always grew in intensity as I approached the front door. After entering the living room I would remain attentive, but the fear would quickly dissipate. I knew the importance of simply watching this event without any comment or judgment, because any response at all would distort or redirect what was happening and destroy the purity and the truth of it.

This went on every day for five days and I was really giving my attention to it, but did not have a clue as to its source. I have had other incidents similar to this in the past, and was aware that this fear was and always is just a cover-up, a defensive action for something going on at a deeper level. It is just a matter of being attentive to it without speculating, thinking, or even naming this emotion. If the mind is quiet and attentive, whatever is being observed will complete itself and move on, revealing what is hidden, what is next, and in this case, revealing what was being covered up.

I have little doubt that future behavioral therapies will be greatly enhanced when there is a greater understanding about the value of doing nothing except to stand aside and watch a problem play itself out and reveal its little mysteries.

Meditation to me is not separate from the activities and events that take place in the course of the day. It is through the quiet observation of these events and conflicts as they appear during the day that brings clarity, resolution, and can result in an increasingly meditative state of mind.

As I opened the front door on this fifth day, the living room was a solid block of body-trembling fear. Nevertheless, I held my ground and would not give thought to what was happening. As I entered the house I was drawn to the opening of a closet and knew well enough not to flinch, not to escape, but to face this living, moving thing. I stood there, motionless, while it expressed itself fully.

Because it was not being acknowledged, not interfered with, it reached its height, its tether, and simply could not continue, which is the case with anything being silently observed to its end. Then, like a tightly wrapped blanket, it suddenly lost its grip and the fear fell away completely, leaving a deep, vibrating emptiness, which then slowly filled with the hidden, the unknown, which was a vast and deep loneliness.

This loneliness, I believe, was partially personal, but also had a considerable universal quality to it. It was not so much a personal loneliness as it was the loneliness of all, perhaps the loneliness of mankind, which I am a part of. This perception was imbedded in and accompanied by a great insight into how we are all trapped in time, all seeking ways to avoid the very roots of our problems, because it is so frightening, and is oftentimes accompanied by the feeling of losing control.

The loneliness and insights lasted for several minutes, and as they slipped away, that vacuum was filled with a silent and vibrant joy which lasted into the next day.

Facing the root cause, the bottom line of a crisis, and letting it play out and tell its story will always produce a positive transformation in consciousness. The end result is not only a change in the mind, but also an organic change in the brain itself because the cells which were displaying the critical event, these very brain cells, undergo an immediate mutation and the entire emotional content of the crisis becomes disarmed, leaving an unstressed, disarmed memory trace, just a husk without the corn.

I have spent most of my life — and presently, living and acting as you, the reader — in the field of time where memory is the dominate factor in the perceptions of the day. I have been fortunate, however, in that the action of meditation in the past forty years has brought about considerable resolution to many conflicts and has produced a fairly smooth and enjoyable life. There also has been a high capacity to resolve and dissipate many of the stresses and distractions now presented to us by the modern world. What has been discovered will be kept, despite deterioration in the brain due to aging.

To the question, "What would be the most important part of every day?" I would say to be watchful to what is going on inside and outside and to see your inward response to various activities and the movement of thought and not to comment on any of it, not even to name or label the activity. It is the naming of it, the acknowledgment of it, which gives further life to it and keeps it alive. That inward response is the movement of old memory, and when that happens you can see the trap that you have built for yourself. You will see the prison of time in action.

So long as time is producing its products of yesterday there can be no timelessness, there can be no newness. You will see, however, that the sporadic intervention of attentiveness will bring about the slowing down of the output of the brain, and as it slows the space between thoughts will increase and a new quietness will come into being. This is meditation in action.

To continue beyond this, complete silence can come into fullness and the door to one's real home may open. Some call this the gate to heaven. This will have happened not by you, but by the nature of the attentiveness itself, which is to me the Greater Friend, the sentry at the gate. It is timeless and free of that fragment of thought called *I*. It is eternal, it is the source of all that there is. It is absolute.

Most of us have perhaps heard the now old saying, "Let there be peace in the world and let it begin with me." Perhaps world peace will require divine intervention. I most respectfully suggest that you are the divine! You are the one to intervene! You can change your world. You can change the world.

Whether you, the reader, are 19 or 99, I would assure you that you will live long enough to discover the truth of these things. It's really up to you.

Whether one understands this phenomenon or not, lives will come and lives will go and this thing which is your silent supporter, your root cause and the background to your very existence, will endlessly remain and be seen at a time when there becomes an active interest or an inward demand to find out.

The most valuable discovery for myself is this space between thought, where duality cannot reside and wherein lies the key to self-discovery, including the death of the illusionary *I*, and freedom from the past. This space is the expandable window into eternity for all, and all that there is.

www.ingramcontent.com/pod-product-compliance
Lightning Source LLC
Chambersburg PA
CBHW060510030426
42337CB00015B/1835